My Little Catechism

Nihil Obstat: Rev. Matthew Ernest, s.t.d.
Censor Librorum

Imprimatur: ✠ His Eminence, Timothy Cardinal Dolan
Archbishop of New York
May 4, 2016

My Little Catechism

Text by
Father Guillaume de Menthière

Illustrations by
Emilie Vanvolsem

MAGNIFICAT · Ignatius

Contents

PART 2: Jesus the Savior

PART 3: The Holy Spirit in the Church

Introduction

What is a catechism?

Like an echo in the mountains, a **catechism** makes the Word of God ring within us to change our lives. We are surrounded by so many useless words that change nothing, that are just chatter. But the Word of God is a Word that changes everything. It is like a jackhammer breaking up our hearts of stone! In order to hear this Word, it is not enough just to listen to it: we must also let it echo within us.

The Word of God is no ordinary word. The Word of God is a Someone! Saint John tells us that **Jesus is the Word**, which means the Word is a person! Everything that God has to say to us, he says by giving us his Son, Jesus. This catechism helps us learn more about Jesus so that we can know him, follow him, and keep him always in our hearts.

The Bible says: *So shall my word be that goes forth from my mouth; it shall not return to me empty, but it shall accomplish that which I intend, and prosper in the thing for which I sent it.* (Isaiah 55:11)

We believe: Jesus is everything God wishes to tell us. He is the Word of God. This catechism will help this Word to echo in our hearts.

Put it into practice: Be silent! You are often asked to do that. But if you are asked to be quiet in church or during prayer, it is not to keep the noise down: it is so that you can hear the Word of God.

🕯 My prayer: Virgin Mary, you who kept the Word in your heart, help me to hear the Word in this catechism. Hail Mary…

❓ Test yourself: What word does a catechism teach us? Who is called the Word?

How can we know Jesus?

We can know Jesus through the **Holy Scriptures** in the Bible. The books of the Bible were written before and after Jesus. They were collected together by the successors to the Apostles, the bishops of the Catholic Church. **Tradition** is the handing down of the Word of God entrusted to the Apostles. Guided by the Holy Spirit, the Church makes sure there is no error or omission in what is handed down. The Church faithfully teaches us the Word of God through the pope and the bishops. The Church is at the same time our mother and our teacher.

The Bible says: *Guard the truth that has been entrusted to you by the Holy Spirit who dwells within us.* (2 Timothy 1:14)

We believe: We can know Jesus, the Word of God, through the Scriptures and through the Tradition that has been faithfully handed down to us, under the watchful care of the Magisterium.

Put it into practice: Do you own a Bible? If not, perhaps your parents or your brother or sister may have one. Page through the Bible respectfully to start your discovery of the Word of God.

My prayer: Blessed are you, Lord, for your Church that has faithfully handed down the Holy Scriptures to us. Teach me to discover them.

Test yourself: What is the book of the Holy Scriptures called? What is Tradition?

3

What is the Bible?

The Bible is one thick book made of seventy-three smaller books. Almost a whole library! It has two parts: the **Old Testament**, the history of the people of Israel to whom the coming of Christ was foretold, and the **New Testament**, which contains the **four Gospels**, the most important stories about Jesus, and the writings of his first disciples. Christians love the Holy Scriptures, as they love anything that has to do with Jesus. They believe the Holy Spirit *has spoken through the prophets*, that the Spirit of God is the principal author of the Bible and inspired the men who wrote it. The Church guards the Bible like a treasure, never letting a single word get lost.

The Bible says: *Men moved by the Holy Spirit spoke from God.* (2 Peter 1:21)

We believe: The whole Bible, which contains the Old and the New Testaments, is inspired by the Holy Spirit and speaks to us of Jesus.

Put it into practice: In your Bible, try to find the Old and the New Testaments. Can you tell how many books there are in the New Testament?

My prayer: Jesus, a loving heart can find you in every page of the Bible. Grant that I may eagerly seek you!

Test yourself: What are the two parts of the Bible? Who is the principal author of the Holy Scriptures?

4

What is the Creed?

The early Church wrote a kind of summary of the Christian faith: the **Apostles' Creed**. It is a short text said by the baptized to show that they share the faith of the Church. It is called the Apostles' Creed because it sums up the faith of Jesus' twelve Apostles, who were the leaders of the Church. This text is also called the **Credo** (*credo* means "I believe" in Latin.) It is the basis for this catechism. We say the Apostles' Creed, or a longer form called the Nicene Creed, at Sunday Mass.

The Bible says: *The word is very near you; it is in your mouth and in your heart, so that you can do it.* (Deuteronomy 30:14)

We believe: The Apostles' Creed unites all Christians who share the faith handed down by the Apostles of Jesus.

✝ **Put it into practice:** Copy the Apostles' Creed. Read it every day until you know it by heart.

🕯 **My prayer:** Lord, I do not yet understand everything, but I believe what the Church tells me in the Apostles' Creed. Help me to understand it better and better.

❓ **Test yourself:** When do we say the Apostles' Creed? What other name do we call the Apostles' Creed?

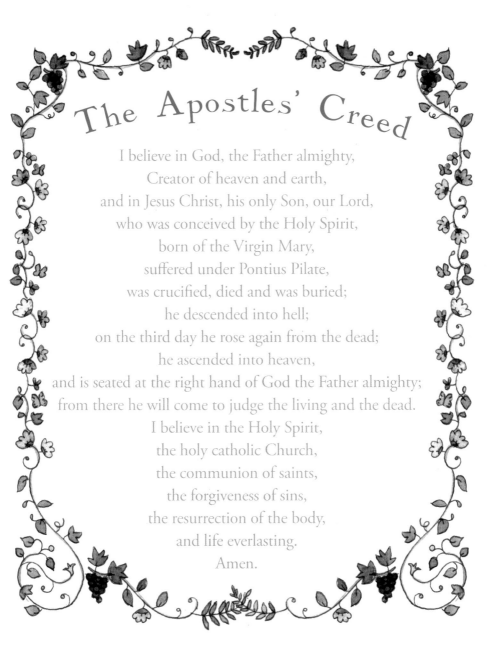

The Apostles' Creed

I believe in God, the Father almighty,
Creator of heaven and earth,
and in Jesus Christ, his only Son, our Lord,
who was conceived by the Holy Spirit,
born of the Virgin Mary,
suffered under Pontius Pilate,
was crucified, died and was buried;
he descended into hell;
on the third day he rose again from the dead;
he ascended into heaven,
and is seated at the right hand of God the Father almighty;
from there he will come to judge the living and the dead.
I believe in the Holy Spirit,
the holy catholic Church,
the communion of saints,
the forgiveness of sins,
the resurrection of the body,
and life everlasting.
Amen.

PART 1
The Father Creator

5

Does God exist?

If you go for a walk in the forest and see a stack of wood, you know that someone has been there and piled up this wood. The wood did not stack itself, just by chance. If you look at the universe: the sky, the stars, the cycle of the seasons, the wonderful shape of a rose, an insect, and, above all, a human being, you again understand that someone has done all that. We call that someone God.

In this way, wise men, philosophers, discovered the existence of God. But, so that everyone could know him, **God revealed himself**: he spoke to Abraham, he taught his name to Moses, and he fully made himself known in his Son, Jesus Christ.

The Bible says: *Lord, how manifold are your works! In wisdom you have made them all.* (Psalms 103 (104): 24)

We believe: Just as a painter reveals himself through his artwork, God reveals himself through everything he makes. We can know God by looking at the order and the beauty in the universe—from the largest galaxy to the smallest atom.

Put it into practice: Look at a beautiful painting. Did someone paint it, or did it paint itself? What does it say about the person who painted it? What does the beauty of creation tell us about God?

My prayer: We give you thanks, Lord, for your great glory, which reveals itself in the universe you created!

Test yourself: How can we discover God? Who best helps us to know God?

What does it mean to believe in God?

To believe in God is not just to know that he exists. Above all, it is **to trust in him**, to listen to his Word, and to follow him in everything, even if that means making changes in our lives. Through the **virtue of faith**, your mind and your will unite with God. It is not easy to see the truth and to have trust: that is why God helps us. No one can have faith without the help of God, which we call **grace**.

Faith is not just words or ideas. It is also actions. The best proof for a cook that you've enjoyed his meal is not your compliments, but an empty plate and the smile on your face! We prove our trust in God, not just through words, but by doing his will. This is how faith produces **works of faith**.

The Bible says: *Without faith it is impossible to please God. For whoever would draw near to God must believe that he exists and that he rewards those who seek him.* (Hebrews 11:6)

We believe: Faith is the gift of God that helps us to know him and to trust him.

Put it into practice: It is said that the crocodile never stops growing from the moment it is born to the moment it dies. Draw a picture of a crocodile and color it in a little every day to remind you to ask God for faith that grows bigger each day!

My prayer: Lord, I ask for faith that grows each day until my trust in you knows no bounds!

Test yourself: What is faith? Who helps us to have faith?

Can we know everything about God?

A child was on the beach digging a hole in the sand. Using his bucket, he wanted to pour the whole sea into the hole. He was told, "You're crazy, you can't do that!" Well, just as the ocean cannot fit into a little hole in the sand, all of God cannot fit into our minds! God is too great for that! We say God is a **mystery**, which means a truth that we must seek to know but without ever understanding it completely. We never stop being **seekers of God**!

The Bible says: *If you seek it like silver and search for it as for hidden treasures, then you will understand the fear of the Lord and find the knowledge of God.* (Proverbs 2:4–5)

We believe: God is a mystery. He is so great, we never stop getting to know him. Just like explorers, Christians never tire of discovering the wonders of God.

✝ Put it into practice: Take a swim. Did you know the word "baptism" means "to plunge in"? Through Baptism, you were plunged into the mystery of God. All your life, you will go on discovering the treasures of this infinite ocean! So dive in!

🕯 My prayer: Lord, you are a bottomless well. Make me always thirsty for you!

❓ Test yourself: Can I know God completely ? Why try to know him at all ?

Should we be afraid of God?

The mystery of God makes us feel awe, which is a kind of fear. The **fear of God** is not fright, but a mixture of respect and love.

When you do something wrong, you are *afraid* of being found out. But, when you have done your best, you still *fear* you may not have done well enough. Do you see the difference between being afraid and fear? Jesus often tells us in the Gospels, "**Do not be afraid!**"

The best way to know God is to love. For, as Saint John tells us, *God is love, he who loves knows God.*

The Bible says: *The fear of the Lord delights the heart, and gives gladness and joy and long life.* (Sirach 1:12)

We believe: The fear of God is the beginning of wisdom; it helps us to love and know God.

✝ Put it into practice: Look at a starry sky. How beautiful it is, and how awesome! You are full of wonder. Fear of God is a bit like that.

🕯 My prayer: Lord, I am little and you are immense, but I am not frightened, for I know that you love me.

❓ Test yourself: Is there a difference between being afraid and fear? What is the best way to know God?

Who is God?

In order to understand who God is, imagine a musician. A musician is not a note of music or a nice sound. He is the source of the music, but he is a human being and not the music itself.

In the same way, God, who is the origin of all that exists, cannot be compared to anything that exists. This is why we say he is the **wholly Other**. He does not have some abilities as we do: he is the **Almighty**, which means he is all-powerful. *Nothing is impossible for God.* Unlike everyone and everything we know, he does not have a single flaw: he is perfect. He is **eternal**, without beginning or end. He is **spirit**. He is not limited to this place or that: his majesty fills the universe and even goes beyond it.

The Bible says: *It is always in your power to show great strength, and who can withstand the might of your arm?* (The Wisdom of Solomon 11:21)

We believe: God is a spirit, eternal, infinite, and perfect, the master of all. He is beyond the most wonderful thing we can imagine. This is why he is called the wholly Other.

Put it into practice: Read one of the miracle stories in the Gospels (for example, the story of the paralytic in Mark 2:1-12). How does Jesus show he is the almighty God?

My prayer: My God, since you can do anything, make me a saint!

Test yourself: To what can God be compared? Since when does God exist?

What is the mystery of the Trinity?

In the Gospels, Jesus speaks to us about God the Father and calls him *Abba* ("Daddy"). He also says, "The Father and I are one." The Father and the Son love one another so very much that their shared love is infinite, and this shared love is called the Holy Spirit. Thus, **the Father, the Son, and the Holy Spirit** are perfectly united. They are distinct yet inseparable. The three of them are one God. This is what we call the mystery of the **Trinity**. Christian believe in only one true God, who is a perfect communion of love between three Persons: the Father, the Son, and the Holy Spirit. What a wonderful thing to know that God is love!

The Bible says: *Jesus saw the heavens opened and the Spirit descending upon him like a dove; and a voice came from heaven, "You are my beloved Son; with you I am well pleased."* (Mark 1:10-11)

We believe: I believe in one God who is a perfect communion of love between three infinite Persons: the Father, the Son, and the Holy Spirit. This is the mystery of the Holy Trinity.

Put it into practice: A little grammar! You were baptized "in the name of the Father, and of the Son, and of the Holy Spirit." Is the word "name" singular or plural? They are three, but they have just one name, for they are one single God!

My prayer: O my God, Trinity whom I adore, let me abide in you, still and peaceful as if my soul were already in eternity. (Blessed Elizabeth of the Trinity)

Test yourself: How did Jesus address his Father? How many gods do Christians worship?

Why did God create the universe?

God has always existed. He has always been the Father, Son, and Holy Spirit, overflowing with love. And so he had no need to create anything to be happy and to love. But he wanted us to share in his joy. God freely wished to **create** all things *so that many might rejoice in his light*. Because, when one is full of love, one wishes to share it.

Before God created the world, there was no time and no space. It is impossible for us to imagine, but there was absolutely nothing except God. We say that God created everything **ex nihilo**, which means "out of nothing". God said, "Let there be light!" and there was light. *He spoke and it came into existence, he commanded and it came to pass.*

The Bible says: *In the beginning God created the heavens and the earth.... And God saw that it was good.* (Genesis 1:1-10)

We believe: To communicate his joy and his love, God freely created all things out of nothing.

Put it into practice: Be full of wonder! Can you count the number of the stars? Can you count the grains of sand on the beach? God made all of that, from the infinitely great to the infinitely small!

My prayer: O Lord, our God, how great is your name through all the universe!

Test yourself: Did God have to create anything? Did God have anything to use for his creation?

What is the invisible world?

Dogs can pick up a scent and hear noises that you cannot even notice. You know that there are lots of things that your eyes cannot see, that your nose cannot smell, that completely escape your five senses. God created that invisible world as well as all visible things. Among the beings that you cannot see, but whom God also created, are the **angels**. You do not see them because they do not have a body; they are pure spirit. Like us, they can serve God or oppose him.

The angels who oppose God are called demons. They have a leader, whom we call the **devil** or **Satan**. Seeking to harm us, they tempt us to disobey God.

The spirits who faithfully serve God are the **good angels**. They worship the Lord and sing his praise in heaven. They come to our aid, and each of us has a special **guardian angel**. Angels also serve as messengers of God. Perhaps you have heard about the archangels Michael, Raphael, and Gabriel, who are in the Bible.

The Bible says: *Then the devil left Jesus, and behold, angels came and ministered to him.* (Matthew 4:11)

We believe: God created the angels. Some rebelled against him: they are the demons. The others obeyed him: they are the good angels. Among the good angels are our guardian angels who watch over us.

Put it into practice: Do you know that you can talk to your guardian angel? Ask him to help you.

My prayer: O my guardian angel, teach me to be faithful to God, watch over me, and protect me from all harm.

Test yourself: Can we see angels? What do we call the bad angels who oppose God?

What is providence?

Your parents gave birth to you, but they did not stop there: they take care of you to make sure you grow and thrive. Just imagine how God, who is a whole lot better than any parent in the world, takes care of his creation! He never stops providing for it, protecting it, and leading it to its goal. **Providence** is God's extraordinary care for every created thing, from the biggest planet to the tiniest insect! Along with the three young men in the Bible (Daniel 3), we can invite all creatures to praise God: *Bless the Lord, sun and moon; and you, birds of the air, bless the Lord; and you, beasts and cattle, bless the Lord!…*

The Bible says: *Who has begotten the drops of dew?* (Job 38:28)

We believe: God, Creator and Lord of all things, is provident. He takes care of creation with wisdom and through love.

Put it into practice: Do a good deed. When you do a good deed (help someone, share what you have, give of your time, visit someone lonely), you are taking part in divine providence.

My prayer: The Lord is my shepherd, I fear no evil. He leads me to green pastures, he gives me rest near peaceful waters. (Based on Psalm 23)

Test yourself: Who provides for all of my needs? Who created the ostrich, the whale, the stars? How can I take part in God's providence for others?

How did God create man and woman?

After creating the earth, the sea, the sky, and all the plants and the animals, God said, "Let us make man and woman **in our image, after our likeness**, that they may reign over the animals, the fish, the birds, and all other creatures." The Bible tells how God molded a human being from dust, as a potter does with clay. Then, with the breath of life, he gave him a soul, which means an immortal spirit.

So a human being has a **body** and a **soul**. It is our souls that have knowledge and will, which give us the possibility to be free and the ability to love.

The Bible says: *You have made man little less than the angels, and you have crowned him with glory and honor. You have given him dominion over the works of your hands; you have put all things under his feet.* (Psalms 8:5-6)

We believe: Man and woman were created in the image of God to reign over all visible creation and to make this gift of God fruitful. God gave them a body and a soul, through which they resembled their Creator, having, like him, the power to love.

Put it into practice: Do good to your soul. You nourish your body each day with food. Did you know that there is also food for the soul? By praying, listening to the Word of God, and receiving the Eucharist, you nourish your soul. Don't let it go hungry!

My prayer: Lord, my God, you who placed in my soul the ability to love, let me grow in love so that I may be a little more like you each day.

Test yourself: Why must we respect every human being? How do we resemble God?

What is original sin?

God created the first man and the first woman: **Adam and Eve**. They lived in a wonderful garden, Eden, where God shared his divine life with them. But, tricked by the serpent, Adam and Eve disobeyed God and ate the fruit of the forbidden tree. Because of their pride, they believed that by their own doing they could make themselves like God. From that moment on, lies, jealousy, violence, and death entered the world. God sent Adam and Eve out of the garden; the beautiful creation of God had been spoiled. Since then, people have been born weak and attracted to evil. That is **original sin**: the fall of our first parents and its sad consequences in us.

The Bible says: *The serpent beguiled me, and I ate.* (Genesis 3:13)

We believe: Original sin is the sin of Adam and Eve, who, tempted by the devil, turned away from God and damaged the work of the Creator. Since then, all people, with the exception of Jesus and the Virgin Mary, are wounded by original sin and attracted to evil.

Put it into practice: Make the sign of the cross with holy water and recall that the water of Baptism washed you clean of original sin and made you a child of God.

My prayer: O God, our Father, thank you for making me your son or daughter!

Test yourself: What were the names of our first parents? Who tricked them?

What is sin?

Sin is thinking, saying, or doing something we know is wrong. We can also sin by omission, that is, by refusing to say or to do something we know we should.

Thinking of ways to tease someone, accusing your brother of something you did, not helping, refusing to go to Mass on Sunday—in doing any of these things on purpose we sin, which offends God, hurts others, and harms ourselves.

Killing someone, stealing a lot of money—if done deliberately, these sins are so serious that we call them **mortal sins**, because they turn us away from God, who is the source of life. Stealing a piece of candy on a dare, not finishing a chore because of a distraction, and other lesser sins are called **venial sins**. While not as damaging as mortal sins, venial sins weaken our relationship with God and our ability to act as we should.

The remedy for sin is to be sorry and to ask God for pardon. We do this in the Sacrament of Reconciliation, also called confession.

The Bible says: *Blessed is he whose transgression is forgiven, whose sin is covered!* (Psalms 31 (32):1)

We believe: Sin is an offense against God, who wants what is best for us. It hurts others and ourselves. When we tell the Lord we are sorry for our sins, he forgives us and gives us strength.

Put it into practice: Do an examination of conscience. Ask God to help you to see your sins and to be sorry for them. Think of the bad things you have done on purpose. Think also of what you have not done well. Those are sins. Then go to confession.

My prayer: Have pity on me, my God, in your love. In your great mercy, forgive my sins and give me the strength I need to act as I should.

Test yourself: Are some sins more serious than others? Why? What is the remedy for sin?

After original sin, did God abandon mankind?

One day, the prophet Jeremiah went to visit a potter. He watched him make beautiful vases from clay. When one pot turned out wrong, the potter smashed it and started another. But that is not how God works! When a pot does not turn out right, he takes it back, remodels it, and makes it like new. He fixes it so well that the pot is even more beautiful than before!

God did not abandon mankind after the first sin. Rather he repaired the damage caused by original sin. With God, there is always a way out: we must never lose hope. The

Lord promised that one day **the devil** would be crushed. He sent a Savior to take away our sins and to give us grace.

The Bible says: *I am God and not man, the Holy One in your midst, and I will not come to destroy.* (Hosea 11:9)

We believe: No matter how grave our sin may be, the Lord never abandons us; he loves to forgive and helps us to overcome our faults. The Lord brings good out of evil. Let us place our hope in him.

Put it into practice: Draw a picture. Show the Virgin Mary crushing the serpent underfoot. Mary is the New Eve. Eve let herself be tricked by the devil, but Mary vanquished the devil through the strength of God.

My prayer: O Mary, conceived without sin, pray for us who have recourse to you. (Repeat three times)

Test yourself: Is God faithful? Who leads us the way we should go?

18

What is salvation history?

God is a **good shepherd**. The good shepherd does not abandon the lamb that gets lost. Instead, he goes out looking for it. That takes a bit of time and lots of patience. And that, in a nutshell, is **salvation history**—all the efforts God makes through the ages to rescue his lost lamb.

That little lamb is all of us, it is mankind that has gotten lost and finds itself far from God through sin. The Lord calls to it, he sends his servants to bring it back to him, but the little lamb does not listen, does not want to follow the good shepherd. The Lord increases his blessings. To form a bond with mankind, he makes a **covenant** with Abraham. He renews this through Moses. He sends prophets. And then, finally, he himself comes to seek the lamb, lifts the lamb over his shoulders, nurses it, and brings it back to the sheepfold.

The Bible says: *I myself will search for my sheep, and will seek them out.* (Ezekiel 34:11)

We believe: God repeatedly established and renewed covenants with mankind. He taught us through the prophets, he made known his will, and, finally, he sent his own Son to seek the lost. Such is God's sacred history with us, the history of salvation.

Put it into practice: Some reading. In the Gospels, read these parables: Matthew 21:33-41 and Luke 15:3-7.

My prayer: Lord Jesus, Good Shepherd, you know the little lamb I am: when I get lost in sin, come yourself to find me.

Test yourself: Whom did God send to bring us back to him? What do we call the kind of bond that God made with Abraham, renewed through Moses, and finally established with the new People of God through Jesus?

19

Who is Abraham?

God called Abraham, an elderly man with no children, to enter a covenant with him. God promised to give him a land and a son. **Abraham believed in God**. He left his own country to walk toward the Promised Land. His wife, Sarah, gave birth to Isaac, even though she was very old. What great joy! Yet Abraham loved God more than anything, and when God asked, Abraham freely offered Isaac. Amazed at Abraham's obedience, God promised him that he would be the father of descendants more numerous than the stars in the sky!

And, indeed, Isaac had a son, Jacob (also called **Israel**), who in turn had twelve sons. These twelve sons gave birth to the twelve tribes that formed the **people of Israel**. God kept his promise. Abraham stands at the head of an enormous family, the family of all those who believe in the God of Abraham, Isaac, and Jacob, who will one day live close to God in the Promised Land of Heaven, the land of the living.

The Bible says: *I will indeed bless you, and I will multiply your descendants as the stars of heaven and as the sand which is on the seashore.* (Genesis 22:17)

We believe: God spoke to our father Abraham. All those who believe in God are children of Abraham, on the march toward God's Promised Land.

Put it into practice: Make a family tree. Put Abraham and Sarah at the roots, then look in the Bible (or on the Internet, or ask your catechism teacher) for the names of their child, their grandchildren, and their great-grandchildren.

My prayer: Blessed are you, Lord, in your servant Abraham, the father of all those who believe in you. Grant me the grace to be a child of Abraham by listening to your Word, obeying your commandments, and having trust in you.

Test yourself: What did God promise to Abraham? What is Jacob's other name?

What is the Jewish Passover?

A very long time after Abraham, the **Hebrews**—the people of Israel—were slaves in the land of Egypt. God saw the sufferings of his people and sent **Moses** to deliver them from the hands of Pharaoh, the king of Egypt. As Moses asked them, the people ate a special meal: lamb with unleavened bread. They put the blood of the lambs on their doorposts so that the Lord would **pass over** their homes as he punished the Egyptians. Pharaoh finally let the Hebrews go, but then he pursued them with his army. The Lord parted the Red Sea so that his people could cross it safely, but the Egyptians chasing after them were drowned. Each year, the Jewish people celebrate their liberation from slavery with the **feast of Passover**. Like their ancestors, they eat **paschal lamb** with unleavened bread.

The Bible says: *Moses stretched his hand over the sea; and the Lord drove the sea back by a strong east wind all night, and the waters were divided. And the sons of Israel went into the sea on dry ground.* (Exodus 14:21-22)

✝ **Put it into practice:** Make a map. Show where Egypt is, the Nile River, the Red Sea, the Promised Land.

☕ **My prayer:** Blessed are you, Lord, who wish to free me from my selfishness, from my fears, from my sins, from everything that keeps me from being free.

❓ **Test yourself:** Who led the people in the name of God? What do the people of Israel eat to celebrate Passover?

21

What are the Ten Commandments?

The departure of the Hebrews from Egypt is called the **Exodus**. After they crossed the Red Sea, the people walked for forty years through the desert. God fed them with bread from heaven, called **manna**. This word means

"What is it?" in Hebrew. Manna appeared every morning as a thin layer on the ground, like solid dew. But God did not stop there! He taught his people **true freedom**. Being free means not being ruled by false masters (jealousy, pride, etc.) but following the Lord who loves us. To help his people to follow him, God gave them the law. He gave Moses two stone tablets engraved with the **Ten Commandments**, which sum up the law. On that day, God made a covenant with his people: "If you observe my commandments, *I will be your God and you shall be my people.*"

Let's learn the Ten Commandments

1. You shall worship the Lord your God and him only shall you serve.
2. You shall not take the name of the Lord your God in vain.
3. Remember to keep holy the Lord's Day.
4. Honor your father and your mother.
5. You shall not kill.
6. You shall not commit adultery.
7. You shall not steal.
8. You shall not bear false witness.
9. You shall not covet another person's husband or wife.
10. You shall not covet your neighbor's goods.

The Bible says: *These words which I command you this day shall be upon your heart.* (Deuteronomy 6:6)

We believe: God made a covenant with his people. He made his will known to them by giving them the law and the Ten Commandments.

Put it into practice: Make the two tablets of the law from two pieces of cardboard. Copy down five of the commandments on each of them.

My prayer: Thank you, Lord, for making us know your will. Grant that I may be faithful to your commandments and never be separated from you.

Test yourself: What does it mean to be free? On what were the Ten Commandments engraved?

22

Who are the prophets?

Sadly, even after all God did for his people, they went on sinning: they stole, killed, broke their promises, and worshipped other gods. They broke the covenant that God had made with them. But God, who is slow to anger and rich in love, sent them **prophets** to ask them to return to him. The four great prophets are Isaiah, Jeremiah, Ezekiel, and Daniel. But alas, that was still not enough. So God then said he was going to send a **Savior, the Messiah,** and to establish a **new covenant**. This time, he would not write his commandments on tablets of stone, but directly on the hearts of believers through the Holy Spirit.

The Bible says: *I will put my law within them and write it upon their hearts; and I will be their God and they shall be my people.* (Jeremiah 31:33)

We believe: The prophets spoke on behalf of God to call the people to return to the Lord. They announced the new covenant that God was going to establish by sending a Savior and speaking directly through the Holy Spirit to the hearts of believers.

Put it into practice: Make a list of the prophets. There are four major ones, but there are also twelve others. Look them up in the Bible.

My prayer: Holy Spirit, you who spoke through the prophets, speak to me so that I might return to God with all my heart and soul.

Test yourself: Is God patient? Where did God promise to write his law?

23

Who is the Messiah?

To govern his people, God promised to send an even greater king than **David**, the good king of Israel who loved God and wrote prayers to be sung, the psalms. This new king would be both a descendant of David and the Son of God. In the Old Testament, when a king was chosen, oil was poured over his head: this lovely gesture is called **anointing**. However, God promised to anoint the new king by the Holy Spirit. That is why he would be called the **Messiah**, or in Greek the **Christ**, which means the "Lord's anointed". For almost a thousand years, the people awaited and desired the coming of this promised Messiah. And this promised Messiah would be Jesus Christ.

The Bible says: There shall come forth a shoot from the stump of Jesse [the father of David].... And the Spirit of the LORD shall rest upon him. (Isaiah 11:1-2)

We believe: God promised to send his people a new king from the family of David. The new promised king would be anointed by the Holy Spirit. That is why we call him the Messiah or the Christ.

Put it into practice: A psalm. Write a prayer or a poem to the Lord, as David did. If you are musical, you could sing it or play it on an instrument.

My prayer: Thank you, Lord, for the Holy Spirit, whom I received on the day of my Baptism. Never let me forget that I am a Christian, because through Christ I have been anointed by the Holy Spirit.

Test yourself: What does the word "Messiah" mean? From which family would come the great king promised by God?

PART 2
Jesus the Savior

24

Why is Mary called the Immaculate Conception?

Who could be the mother of the Messiah? For this wonderful mission, in the village of Nazareth, God prepared a totally pure young woman named Mary. She was *full of grace* because she was conceived "immaculate", meaning without the stain of original sin. She is the **Immaculate Conception**, whose feast day is December 8. On seeing the goodness of the Virgin Mary, God sent the angel Gabriel to ask her to be the mother of the Savior. The Virgin replied: "Oh, yes! Let it happen (in Latin, *Fiat*). I am the servant of the Lord." At that very moment, the Holy Spirit came upon her and conceived within her the child Jesus, who was to be her son and the Son of God. He would be a man with a body and a soul like ours, and he would be God, the second Person of the Trinity. How could that come about? It is the great **mystery of the Incarnation**, the mystery of the Son of God made man.

The Bible says: *Hail, full of grace, the Lord is with you!* (Luke 1:28)

Put it into practice: Make an act of obedience to God, like the Virgin Mary, who teaches us to say yes.

My prayer: Hail Mary, full of grace, the Lord is with thee. Blessed art thou among women, and blessed is the fruit of thy womb, Jesus.

Test yourself: Why is Mary said to be immaculate? Is Jesus both the Son of God and the son of the Virgin Mary?

25

What is Christmas?

A very long time ago, the Lord promised through the prophet Isaiah that a young virgin would conceive and give birth to a son who would be "**Emmanuel**, God-with-us". The Lord's promise was fulfilled when the Virgin Mary gave birth to her son, who is God living among us. His name is **Jesus**, which means "God saves", for he is the Savior of the world. On **Christmas** we celebrate the night Jesus was born in a stable in Bethlehem, which means "house of Bread". Later on, Jesus would say, "I am the bread that has come down from heaven." Angels appeared to nearby shepherds, telling them about the newborn Savior in a manger and singing to the glory of God, and the shepherds went to adore him. Afterward, wise men called **Magi** came from the East bearing gifts for the Christ Child. We celebrate their arrival on the feast of the **Epiphany**.

The Bible says: *[Mary] gave birth to her first-born son and wrapped him in swaddling clothes and laid him in a manger, because there was no place for them in the inn.* (Luke 2:7)

Put it into practice: List the names of Jesus. Write all the names for him you know: Son of God, Savior, Light of the World, Good Shepherd, etc.

My prayer: Glory to God in the highest and peace on earth to all good men!

Test yourself: Where was Jesus born? What do we celebrate on the feast of the Epiphany?

26

What was Jesus' childhood like?

After the visit of the Magi, Joseph, Mary, and Jesus, the **Holy Family**, hurriedly fled to Egypt to escape King Herod, who wanted to kill the child. After the king's death, they returned to Nazareth, where Jesus led a **hidden life** until he was thirty years old. Jesus was obedient to his parents, the Virgin Mary and Saint Joseph, and he learned his father's trade of carpentry. Jesus prayed a lot and spoke to God, calling him *Abba*, which means "Daddy". Mary's son was God, so that made her the **Mother of God**! The Virgin could not understand all these wonders, and she humbly and quietly pondered them in her heart.

The Bible says: *Mary kept all these things, pondering them in her heart.* (Luke 2:19)

We believe: Jesus' mission was to save the world. He began by spending thirty years in a hidden life in Nazareth, with his adoptive father, Joseph, and the Virgin Mary, his mother, the Mother of God.

✝ **Put it into practice:** Reflect on the stories of Christ's birth and childhood in the Gospels: Matthew 1:18–2:23 and Luke 1:26-56; 2:1-52. Make a crèche with cardboard, or with wood if you can, in remembrance of Jesus who worked with wood for thirty years.

🕯 **My prayer:** Holy Mary, Mother of God, pray for us sinners, now and at the hour of our death. Amen.

❓ **Test yourself:** Why is the Virgin Mary called the Mother of God? Until what age did Jesus live a hidden life in Nazareth?

27

What did Jesus do during the three years of his public life?

When Jesus was thirty, he asked John the Baptist to baptize him. Then he traveled all over Israel, telling people to change their hearts, to **repent** of their sins, and to live as children of God. He spoke of the **Kingdom of heaven**, and to help people to understand it, he told little stories: the **parables**.

He called the disciples and chose **twelve Apostles**. With them, he went from village to village, announcing the **Gospel**, the **Good News** of salvation, to everyone he met, especially the poor. He welcomed sinners and forgave them, and he challenged the self-righteous. Crowds followed him, for he spoke wonderfully and performed **miracles**. For example, he multiplied loaves of bread, changed water into wine, walked on water, gave sight to the blind, healed the sick, and even raised the dead! Yet, as the people cheered him, he would withdraw to the mountains to spend time **in prayer** with God, his Father.

The Bible says: *Jesus came into Galilee, preaching the gospel of God.* (Mark 1:14)

We believe: During his public life, Jesus taught; he called disciples; he welcomed the poor and sinners; he worked miracles; and, above all, he prayed.

✝ **Put it into practice:** Look up a miracle story or a parable in the Bible. Read it and then tell it to others around you. (Suggestions: Luke 13:6-9, the parable of the barren fig tree; Mark 4:33-41, the miracle of the calming of the storm.)

🕯 **My prayer:** Lord Jesus, you who prayed to God your Father, teach us how to pray, saying: "Our Father…"

❓ **Test yourself:** Why did Jesus tell parables? What was Jesus' attitude toward the poor and sinners?

28

Why was Jesus condemned to death, when he was innocent?

Jesus had many enemies! Among them were those who thought they were better than everyone else. Some of these were Pharisees, men who knew the law of Moses very well and tried to practice it to the letter. Jesus often criticized their pride. Then there were the rich and powerful, because the crowds wanted to make Jesus their king and that threatened their position. Some Jews thought Jesus was committing a terrible sin by calling himself the Son of God, which was like saying he was God himself. Some of the Romans were worried because Jesus stirred up the people and disturbed the peace. All these and more were united in seeking the death of Christ.

Jesus knew that the mission he had received from his Father would lead to his death, which he willingly accepted. "No one takes my life from me," he said to his Apostles, "but I lay it down of my own accord." This is the mystery of **Redemption**. Jesus gave up his life freely, even though he was innocent, to **redeem** us, who are guilty. He made this **sacrifice** for our salvation. Sinners that we are, he loved us to the end.

The Bible says: *The Son of man came not to be served but to serve, and to give his life as a ransom for many.* (Mark 10:45)

We believe: The mystery of Redemption is the ransom for our sinful lives through the sacrifice of Christ, who, though innocent, gave his life freely to save us.

Put it into practice: A sacrifice. Jesus gave his life for us; what can we give to him?

My prayer: Thank you, Lord, for having given your life for us, who do not deserve it. Thank you for loving us that much. Grant us to love you in return with all our heart.

Test yourself: Who wanted the death of Jesus? Did Jesus know that he would be killed?

What is Holy Thursday?

On the evening of Holy Thursday, Jesus knew he was about to die. He wanted to have one last meal with his friends, the Apostles. It was near or during the time of the Jewish feast of Passover, and this meal is called the **Last Supper**. Before the meal, Jesus washed his Apostles' feet and gave them the **great commandment**: "Love one another as I have loved you." Then he took the bread and wine, and offered his life, saying: "This is my Body, this is my Blood, do this in memory of me." Faithful to his words, the Church celebrates **Mass in memory of him.**

After the meal, Jesus and his Apostles went to a garden to pray. Jesus was truly sad at the thought of dying. His sweat became drops of blood: this was the **agony** of the Lord. But his love for God and for us was so great that he did not back away, but freely accepted doing the will of his Father.

When Judas, the Apostle who betrayed Jesus, arrived with armed men, Jesus allowed them to arrest him, without trying to defend himself.

The Bible says: *I have earnestly desired to eat this Passover with you before I suffer.* (Luke 22:15)

We believe: In celebrating the Mass, the Church repeats the words Jesus spoke during the Last Supper on Holy Thursday, according to the Lord's command.

Put it into practice: Do you know how to set the table for dinner? Would you know how to prepare the altar for Mass? List what you would need.

My prayer: Lord, you wished to share the Last Supper with your disciples, and you invite me to participate in your sacrifice at Mass. Help me to respond to your wish by going faithfully to Mass.

Test yourself: What did the Lord do during his last meal? What is the name of the Apostle who betrayed his Master?

30

What is Good Friday?

From his agony on Holy Thursday to his death on Good Friday, Jesus suffered his **Passion**. After his arrest, the Jewish leaders condemned him to death. The disciples had fled, and through fear, Peter denied his Master three times before the cock crowed. The Jewish leaders took Jesus to the Roman governor Pontius Pilate and demanded his execution. Pilate resisted and had Jesus flogged instead, and his soldiers mocked Jesus, placing a crown of thorns on his head. After the crowd called for the death of Jesus, Pilate finally ordered his death on a cross, called crucifixion. Then Jesus carried his heavy cross up the hill of **Calvary** (or Golgotha). There the soldiers nailed him to the cross. While he was suffering horribly, Jesus entrusted his mother, the Virgin Mary, to his Beloved Disciple, so that she would be his mother and the mother of us all. Jesus died on Good Friday at three o'clock in the afternoon, saying: "Father, forgive them, they know not what they do." Each time we celebrate Mass, we take part in the sacrifice of Jesus on the cross and proclaim his death and Resurrection.

The Bible says: *Jesus, remember me when you come in your kingly power.* (Luke 23:42)

We believe: Jesus suffered his Passion and death through love for God and for us. He gave his life in sacrifice and died on the cross to forgive us our sins.

Put it into practice: Make a cross. You can make it out of wood or cardboard. It is the sign of Christians, for Jesus turned this instrument of suffering into the great sign of a love more powerful than anything.

My prayer: Lord, you who suffered so, have mercy on all those who suffer; be their consolation and give them your strength.

Test yourself: Why do we say that the Virgin Mary is our Mother? Why is the Mass said to be the sacrifice of Jesus?

31

Why do we say that Jesus was buried and "descended into hell"?

At the foot of the cross stood the Virgin Mary and Saint John, along with two other women. With the help of Nicodemus, a Pharisee, and Joseph of Arimathea, they placed Jesus' body in a tomb near Golgotha. That is how he was **buried** on the evening of Good Friday.

But Jesus' soul, united to his divine Person, went to deliver the souls of those who had died before him. He **descended into hell**, the dwelling of the dead. For indeed, before Jesus rose from the dead and opened the gates of heaven, the souls of the dead were like prisoners in a place separated from God. Christ smashed the gates of that prison and brought all the **souls of the just of ages past** with him into heaven (for example, Abraham, Sarah, King David, and John the Baptist). On **Holy Saturday**, Christians remember the descent of Christ, truly dead, into hell to free the souls of the just.

The Bible says: *They took the body of Jesus and bound it in linen cloths with the spices, as is the burial custom of the Jews.* (John 19:40)

We believe: The body of Jesus was buried in a tomb; his soul descended into hell to free the just souls who had gone before him, to open the gates of heaven for them.

Put it into practice: Think carefully! There are two different meanings of the word "hell". One is the place where the dead of olden times awaited the coming of Jesus. The other is the eternal separation from God suffered by those who reject his forgiveness.

My prayer: Lord Jesus, you endured a painful death for the salvation of souls. I pray to you for all the people I know who have died. Please welcome them into heaven.

Test yourself: After Jesus' death, who tended to his body? Whom did Jesus deliver on Holy Saturday? From where?

32

Are we sure that Jesus rose from the dead?

Jesus' tomb was sealed with a large stone and guarded by soldiers. Yet, on **Easter Sunday** (the third day after Good Friday and Holy Saturday), women found the stone rolled away and the body of Jesus missing! The Lord appeared alive to **Saint Mary Magdalene**, then to the Apostles, and to two disciples who recognized him when he broke bread at the inn in **Emmaus**. To Saint Thomas, who would not believe them, Jesus showed the marks left by the nails to prove he was alive among them! He had triumphed over death! For forty days, the risen Jesus appeared to his friends and even to more than five hundred others at one time.

Easter is the greatest feast day of Christians, when we celebrate the **Resurrection of Jesus**, singing **alleluia!** The disciples saw him, touched him, spoke to him, and shared grilled fish with him. Almost all would go as far as giving their lives to attest that Jesus really did rise from the dead: these were the first martyrs.

The Bible says: *This was now the third time that Jesus was revealed to the disciples after he was raised from the dead.* (John 21:14)

We believe: Jesus rose from the dead on Easter; he appeared to his disciples who have testified to it. He triumphed over death! He is alive for ever, alleluia!

Put it into practice: Celebrate! Each Sunday, the Church celebrates the Resurrection of the Lord. So, next Sunday, fill your heart with joy and sing alleluia! Celebrate also Easter itself. Think of ways to make the day extra special: festive decorations, yummy foods, and fun activities you can share with your family.

My prayer: Lord Jesus, you are the resurrection and the life! Like Saint Thomas when he saw you risen, I too proclaim that you are my Lord and my God, alleluia!

 Test yourself: Why do we say that Jesus rose "on the third day"? What is the greatest feast day for Christians?

33

What is the Ascension?

Forty days after Easter, Jesus blessed his disciples and gave them the mission to proclaim the Good News of salvation to all the earth. He told them: "I am with you every day until the end of the world." Then, before their eyes, he rose from the earth to join his Father in heaven. We celebrate this event on the **feast of the Ascension**. Since then, Jesus is **seated at the right hand of the Father**, meaning the best seat in the intimacy of God. But that does not mean he has abandoned us! In heaven, he prays to his Father for us. He left to prepare a place for us in heaven. He did not leave us alone on earth: he sent his Holy Spirit. This way, he is always with us through his Spirit!

And he also left us the Sacrament of the Eucharist. We cannot see him any more with our eyes, but our faith recognizes his presence in the consecrated host.

The Bible says: *As [the Apostles] were looking on, he was lifted up and a cloud took him out of their sight.* (Acts 1:9)

Jesus rose to heaven to rejoin his Father. He is above everything, equal to the Father. He left in order to send us the Holy Spirit and to prepare a place for us in heaven. We celebrate this event on the feast of the Ascension.

✝ Put it into practice: Make an "ascension". You can climb up a hill or "go up" in pilgrimage to a holy site. It could be a special church near your home or a very famous shrine such as Immaculate Conception in Washington, D.C., or Saint Peter's in Rome. Holy places are often found in the heights for it is as though, being closer to the sky, we are closer to God.

My prayer: Jesus, take me in your arms to raise me up toward the Father. Like Saint Thérèse of the Child Jesus, I want you to be my elevator, to make me grow in holiness and to lift me up to God.

Test yourself: After rising up to heaven, what does Jesus do for us? Why do we say that Christ is seated at the right hand of the Father?

34

Should I be afraid of Judgment Day?

Jesus left to rejoin his Father, but he will *come again to judge the living and the dead*. He came the first time as a suffering servant to remove our sins and to offer us the mercy of God. He will come a second time in glory for the **last judgment**. All men and women will then appear before him to receive reward or punishment for what they have done. No one knows when this will take place.

So we must always be ready for the coming of Christ. Before that day, **let us do good**, recognize our sins, and **humbly receive the forgiveness he offers us** so that we need have no fear of his judgment. On the contary, we will look forward to his coming and say: "Come quickly, Lord Jesus!" And on the day of his glorious coming, he will say to us, "Come, O you blessed of my Father, inherit the kingdom prepared for you." Then he will take us with him for ever into the glory of his Father in heaven.

The Bible says: *When the Son of man comes in his glory, and all the angels with him, then he will sit on his glorious throne.* (Matthew 25:31)

We believe: Jesus will come in glory for the last judgment. Everyone will then be repaid for their acts.

Put it into practice: Over the entrance of many churches, especially cathedrals, is an image of the last judgment. Christ is in the center, with the good people to his right and the wicked to his left. Find a picture of the last judgment and pick out the many details.

My prayer: Blessed are you, Lord, who generously offers us forgiveness for our sins so that we may have no fear of the day of judgment.

Test yourself: How can we prepare for the coming of the Lord? When will Jesus come again in glory?

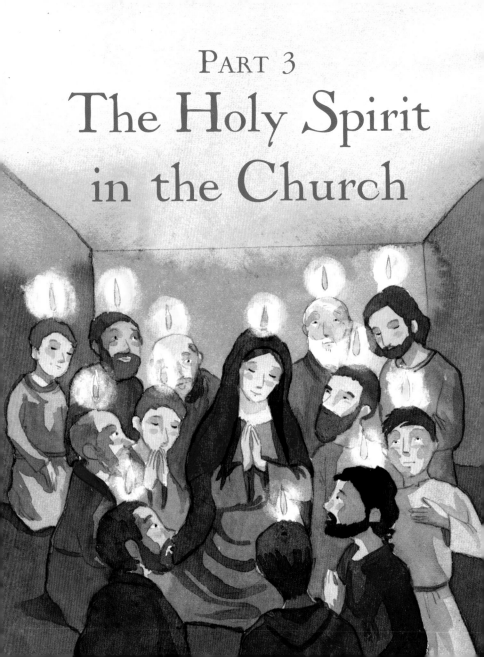

PART 3
The Holy Spirit
in the Church

35

What is celebrated on Pentecost?

On the Jewish feast of **Pentecost**, fifty days after Easter, there was a great gust of wind. The Apostles, gathered together in the **Upper Room** with the Virgin Mary, saw what looked like tongues of fire coming down and settling on each one of them. And they were **filled with the Holy Spirit** that, before he ascended into heaven, Jesus had promised to send them. From then on, they were no longer afraid to share the Good News of the risen Jesus. Peter, the leader of the Apostles, said to the crowd: "Be baptized every one of you, and you shall receive the gift of the Holy Spirit." This is how the Church, the community of those who believe in Christ, grew and spread throughout all the countries in the world.

The Bible says: *There appeared to them tongues as of fire, distributed and resting on each one of them.* (Acts 2:3)

We believe: The Holy Spirit was given to the Apostles on the day of Pentecost, and they went out into the world to proclaim the Good News and to spread the Church.

✝ **Put it into practice:** Look at a calendar. Find the Christian feast days you know: Christmas, Easter, Ascension, Pentecost, etc.

🕯 **My prayer:** Thank you, Lord Jesus, for sending your Holy Spirit to be our comfort and strength and to allow us to know you.

❓ **Test yourself:** Where were the Apostles on the feast of Pentecost? What happened?

36

What does the Holy Spirit do in the Church?

The Holy Spirit is the third Person of the Trinity. He is Lord, equal to the Father and the Son. Through the gift of the Holy Spirit, God's love is poured into our hearts! What does love do? It brings together those who love one another. The Holy Spirit **unites** all Christians in one single Church and keeps them faithful to Jesus Christ. Love also reaches out to those who suffer or are far away. The Holy Spirit **sends** Christians out into the world to bring the Good News of salvation to all men. Love makes us happy. The Holy Spirit brings **joy** to the Church and inspires Christians to praise God in prayer. God wishes all of us to be saints, and that is why he gives us his Spirit. In the Church, some are called to follow a particular path to sainthood in **religious life**. To follow Christ more closely by imitating the way he lived, religious (monks and nuns) make vows of poverty, chastity, and obedience.

The Bible says: *Day by day, attending the temple together and breaking bread in their homes, they partook of food with glad and generous hearts, praising God and having favor with all the people.* (Acts 2:46)

We believe: The Holy Spirit unites Christians, sending them out into the world with the Good News, and inspiring them to praise God.

✝ **Put it into practice:** An anatomy lesson. The Holy Spirit is poured into the body of the Church by Christ who is the head. Like blood flowing in each member, the Holy Spirit makes the Church live and become holy.

🕯 **My prayer:** Holy Spirit, fill my heart with the love of God, make me love the Church and give praise to God with my whole being.

❓ **Test yourself:** What does the Holy Spirit empower Christians to do?

37

What is a sacrament?

The Holy Spirit is *the Lord, the giver of life*. How do we receive the life of God? Through **grace**. Grace is the free gift of God's own life. Our body cannot live without oxygen; in the same way, our soul cannot live without grace. God can offer it to us in many different ways. However, he desires to give grace to us regularly through signs instituted by Jesus, what we call **sacraments**.

When you give a sign of friendship to someone, it often produces a positive reaction: joy, affection, gratitude, etc. The sacraments, Jesus' signs, always produce grace in those who receive them with faith. And so, the wonderful signs that Christ worked in the Gospels continue in the Church through the sacraments: through the Holy Spirit, Jesus continues to heal us, comfort us, forgive us, and nourish us.

The Bible says: *[Jesus] stretched out his hand and touched him, and said to him, "I will it; be clean."* (Mark 1:41)

We believe: The grace of God is given through seven sacred signs instituted by Jesus Christ that we call the sacraments.

Put it into practice: Give your parents a sign of affection. See what effect it produces.

My prayer: Thank you, Lord, for coming into the world to give us your grace through the sacraments. Grant me to receive them with joy as wonderful gifts.

Test yourself: What do we call the gift of God's life? What are the signs instituted by Christ to give us grace?

38

What are the seven sacraments?

The sacraments develop the life of God within us. First comes birth, then nourishment and growth. In the same way, we are born to the life of God through Baptism, we are nourished by the life of God through the Eucharist, and we grow in the life of God through Confirmation (see #40). These first three sacraments are called the **sacraments of initiation**, for they begin in us the life of Christ.

Sometimes life is endangered. For example, when someone is ill or has an accident. In that case, there must be healing and regaining strength. Sin makes our soul sick and wounds it. Then it too needs to be restored. In order for us to regain full health in the life of God, Jesus gave two **sacraments of healing** to his Church: the Sacrament of the Anointing of the Sick and the Sacrament of Penance and Reconciliation (also called confession).

In order for us to live together in harmony, Jesus gave us two **sacraments of service**: the Sacrament of Matrimony, which a man and a woman receive to be married and found a family, and the Sacrament of Holy Orders, received by men to become a deacon, a priest, or a bishop.

The Bible says: *What therefore God has joined together, let no man put asunder.* (Matthew 19:6)

We believe: Jesus instituted seven sacraments: Baptism, Confirmation, Eucharist, Penance and Reconciliation, Anointing of the Sick, Matrimony, and Holy Orders.

✝ Put it into practice: Do a survey. Ask your godfather or your godmother to tell you about your Baptism. Ask your parish priest to tell about his ordination (the ceremony when he received Holy Orders) and ask your parents to tell about their marriage ceremony.

My prayer: Thank you, Lord, for the sacraments that I have already received. Prepare my heart to receive those you still wish to give me.

? Test yourself: What are the other names for the Sacrament of Penance? What do you call the sacrament in which a man becomes a priest?

39

Can we receive the Eucharist whenever we want?

You were born one day, once and for all. On the other hand, to live and to grow, you must have nourishment every day. The Christian too is born just once: on the day of his **Baptism**. But he must nourish himself throughout life with the Word of God and the Body of the Lord, the Eucharist, received at Mass.

When you were a newborn baby, your parents did not give you hamburgers and fries right away! First, they gave you milk. Then, when you got bigger, you ate solid food. In the same way, your faith was first nourished by the milk of the Word of God that you hear at home, at Mass, or in catechism class. This is to prepare you to receive the Body of the Lord in **Communion**.

To be able to receive Communion is not something automatic; you have to be ready for it. It is called to be worthy. The Church also asks that you prepare yourself by fasting for at least an hour before receiving communion.

Before going to receive Communion, take a bit of time to realize that this is truly Jesus present in the Eucharist.

Examine your conscience. While receiving Communion cleanses you from venial sins and helps you not to sin in the future, you should be free from mortal sin when you go to Communion (see #16).

Jesus can heal you through the **Sacrament of Penance and Reconciliation**. After you have confessed your sins, the priest gives the absolution that takes away sin, and you are then required to do a penance, which helps to restore your spiritual health.

The Bible says: *[He] went to him and bound up his wounds, pouring on oil and wine; then he set him on his own beast and brought him to an inn, and took care of him.* (Luke 10:34)

We believe: Like our daily bread, the Eucharist can be received every day as long as we are in good spiritual health. The Sacrament of Penance and Reconciliation can be received as often as necessary to heal us of the sickness of sin.

Put it into practice: Fast. If you go without food, your body will be hungry. If you go without the Body of Christ, your soul will be hungry.

My prayer: Jesus, you said that your Body is true food. Make me hunger for you!

Test yourself: Why can't we receive Baptism several times? Can anybody receive Communion whenever he wants?

40

What does the Holy Spirit do in the hearts of Christians?

The Holy Spirit makes holy all those he breathes upon. The Spirit is like the wind and blows where he wills, spreading the gifts of God everywhere. Yet he especially wishes to live within the baptized as in a temple. From the day of our **Baptism**, we have the Holy Spirit within us. We receive him again along with the fullness of his gifts in the Sacrament of **Confirmation**. It is because we have the **anointing** of the Holy Spirit that we are Christians, meaning other Christs.

The Holy Spirit makes us children of God. He brings us into contact with God by giving us faith, hope, and love (or charity): these are the **three theological virtues**. He gives us the desire and the courage to do what is good and to avoid evil. He leads us to prayer and service and fills us with joy. He offers us seven gifts: wisdom, understanding, counsel, knowledge, fortitude, piety, and fear of God; and many fruits: charity, joy, peace, patience, kindness, goodness, generosity, gentleness, faithfulness, modesty, self-control, and chastity.

The Bible says: *For all who are led by the Spirit of God are sons of God.* (Romans 8:14)

We believe: The Holy Spirit comes to us at Baptism and at Confirmation. He dwells in the hearts of Christians, places the life of God within them, and empowers them to act according to what is right.

Put it into practice: It is very important to keep in shape and to care for your body, because as Saint Paul said: "Did you not know that your body is the temple of the Holy Spirit?" Do some physical exercise and be careful of the way you eat!

My prayer: Holy Spirit, you who live in my soul, grant that I may listen to you and always follow your advice; protect me from bad thoughts and teach me to do what is right.

? Test yourself: Through which sacrament do we receive the fullness of the Holy Spirit? What does the word "Christian" mean?

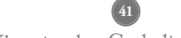

What is the Catholic Church?

Jesus came into the world "to gather into one the children of God who are scattered". This gathering is called the Church. It is like the flock of Jesus, the Good Shepherd. The Lord said to Simon Peter, "Tend my sheep", and, "You are Peter, and upon this rock I will build my church." Today, the pope, Peter's successor, leads the Church of Jesus on earth.

The Church is **catholic**, which means it is universal, because God gave it everything needed to lead us to salvation, and because its purpose is to gather together all men.

The Church is **apostolic**, because it is founded on the Apostles, because it is governed by the bishops, the successors of the Apostles, and because it is sent out to bring the Good News to the world (the word "Apostle" means "sent" in Greek).

The Bible says: You are Peter, and on this rock I will build my Church, and the gates of Hades shall not prevail against it. I will give you the keys of the Kingdom of heaven, and whatever you shall bind on earth shall be bound in heaven, and whatever you loose on earth shall be loosed in heaven. (Matthew 16:18-19)

We believe: The Church gathers together all those whom Jesus saves. She has all the means of salvation and seeks to unite the whole human family, which is why she is called the Catholic Church.

Put it into practice: Do some research. Who is the current pope? Who is your bishop? Pray for them by name.

My prayer: Blessed are you, Lord, for your Church! Give her the joy of growing by welcoming new children of God. Watch over the pope, who guides your Church on earth.

Test yourself: To whom did Jesus entrust the care of the Church? What does the word "catholic" mean?

42

What is the communion of saints?

The Church is **one** and **holy**: it is the **communion of saints**! In the Church, there are we Christians who live on earth and also those who have already died. Some of the faithful departed are in purgatory, where they are prepared for heaven, and some are already in heaven. These three groups of the faithful (**on earth, in purgatory, and in heaven**) are united by the Holy Spirit, the bond of charity. Each of them can come to the others' aid, as when we ask the Virgin Mary or a certain saint to pray for us, or when we pray for those who have died. When we receive Communion at Mass, we are in communion with God and with all who share the same Bread of God. Communion unites Christians in the **Body of Christ**. In a body there is a head and different members (the foot, the hand, the knee, etc.), but all are united to form one single body. It is the same with the Church: there is the Head (Christ), and many different members (priests, children, grandparents, religious, those who have passed away), but they are all united in the communion of saints.

The Bible says: *Now you are the body of Christ and individually members of it.* (1 Corinthians 12:27)

We believe: The Church is the communion of saints that unites into one family the faithful on earth, the souls in purgatory, and the saints in heaven.

Put it into practice: Do some research about your patron saint, the saint whose name you bear. If you are not named after a saint, ask your parents or your parish priest for the saints celebrated the day you were born and choose one of them as your patron saint. Say a prayer to him or her.

My prayer: Lord, today I offer you my prayer and my sacrifices for the souls in purgatory, that you may welcome them into heaven.

Test yourself: What are the three groups of faithful united in the communion of saints? Why is the Church said to be the Body of Christ?

43

What is the forgiveness of sins?

Jesus came to save sinners. After Easter, he breathed on the Apostles, saying to them: "Receive the Holy Spirit. If you forgive the sins of any, they are forgiven; if you retain the sins of any, they are retained." This is how the Church received from Jesus **the power to forgive sins**. The Church forgives sins through the **Sacrament of Baptism**. In the waters of Baptism, the Holy Spirit cleanses us of all sin. The Church forgives sins committed after Baptism through the **Sacrament of Penance and Reconciliation**. A baptized person who is sorry for his sins can confess them to a priest, who gives him a **penance** to perform in order to heal some of the damage caused by sins, followed by **absolution**. The penitent is then forgiven, freed from his guilt, and reconciled with the Lord, whom he had offended by sinning. We believe that the **mercy** of God is so great that all our sins, even the most serious and most frequent, can be forgiven. The forgiveness we freely receive from God, we must also grant generously to others.

The Bible says: *"Lord, how often shall my brother sin against me, and I forgive him? As many as seven times?" Jesus said to him, "I do not say to you seven times, but seventy times seven."* (Matthew 18:21-22)

We believe: The Church received from Jesus the power to forgive sins, which she does principally through the Sacraments of Baptism and of Penance and Reconciliation.

Put it into practice: Make a gesture of forgiveness. Perhaps there is someone who has hurt you or done something bad to you. Offer him your forgiveness. Or if, on the other hand, it is you who have done someone harm, ask him for his forgiveness, and try to repair the harm you have done.

My prayer: Our Father, forgive us our sins as we forgive those who sin against us.

Test yourself: Through which sacrament can a baptized person be forgiven for his sins? Are there any sins that God cannot forgive, if we ask him humbly?

44

When we die, what becomes of our soul and our body?

We are made up of a body and a soul. When we die, **body and soul are separated**. The body is buried and the soul is judged by God: that is called the **particular judgment**. The soul goes to purgatory, heaven, or hell, according to what it merits. In heaven, the souls are fully happy in the joy of God: they are in **paradise**. In **purgatory**, souls are purified by God to become worthy of paradise. In **hell**, souls suffer separation from the God they continue to reject.

When Christ comes in his glory at the end of time, all souls will be reunited with their bodies. This will be the **resurrection of the body**. Your whole being (body and soul) will be whole again for the **last judgment**. In that moment everything God has done will be fulfilled and everything man has done will be fully known. The Virgin Mary is a sign for us. She entered heaven body and soul on the day of her **Assumption**.

The Bible says: *I will open your graves and raise you from your graves, O my people; and I will bring you home into the land of Israel.* (Ezekiel 37:12)

We believe: When Christ comes in his glory, the souls of the deceased will be reunited with their bodies; the elect will enter, body and soul, into paradise, and the damned into hell.

Put it into practice: Visit a cemetery. The bodies of the dead are buried in graves and return to dust. But the Creator God will raise them again at the end of time. Pray for the souls of the departed.

My prayer: Holy Mary, Our Lady of the Assumption, you who are already, body and soul, in paradise with your Son, Jesus, pray for us now and at the hour of our death.

Test yourself: Who is now already, body and soul, in paradise?

45

What is eternal life?

In heaven we will see God and all our desire for happiness will be fulfilled by being in his presence. We do not really know how that will happen, but we do know that we will be **with Jesus**; so it will be fantastic! Jesus is the one whose merits open the gates of heaven for us. But we still must do all we can to get there by confessing our sins, doing the will of God, and receiving the **Eucharist**, for Jesus said, "He who eats my flesh has eternal life, and I will raise him up at the last day." For the rest, we trust in the Lord. When **the end of time** comes, he will make **all things new**, all will be renewed in love, and there will be no mourning, no tears, no hate, no suffering, no death. There will be nothing but the joy of God for all the saints for ever! God's plan will at last be fully realized: that will be **eternal life**!

The Bible says: *Then I saw a new heaven and a new earth.* (Revelation 21:1)

 **We believe:** At the end of time, Jesus will make all things new and the elect will be with him for ever in the Kingdom of God, which knows no death or sin or suffering, but only joy and peace in the Holy Spirit.

✝ **Put it into practice:** Prepare for Communion. When you receive the Eucharistic Jesus within you, ask that, in heaven, you may enjoy for ever a communion of life and love with him.

🕯 **My prayer:** Lord, place within me a great desire to be a saint, so that I may live eternally with you.

❓ **Test yourself:** Will we live for ever on this earth? What does Jesus promise to those who receive his Body in Communion?

46

Is all this really true?

The Apostles' Creed, the "I believe in God", ends with the Hebrew word "amen", a way of saying "solid as a rock". That means we can rely on the faith of the Church and have confidence in Jesus who is the **Truth**. All kingdoms, empires, and nations disappear one after another, even the most powerful and best armed, but the **Church endures**, because she is founded on the rock of the Word of God. And this Word, Jesus said, must be **put into practice**. It is not enough just to believe it!

We must also live by respecting the two great commandments: love God with all your heart, and love your neighbor as yourself. Do that, and you will live in the joy of the children of God!

The Bible says: *That [...] house did not fall, because it had been founded on the rock.* (Matthew 7:25)

We believe: Jesus is the Way, the Truth, and the Life. He is the Word of God, the solid rock upon which Christians rely through faith.

Put it into practice: Recite the following text as an Act of Faith: "O God, I firmly believe all the truths that you have revealed and that you teach through your Church, for you are truth itself and can neither deceive nor be deceived."

My prayer: My God, I have received everything from you. Help me to understand your teaching better and better, and make of my life an offering of praise to your glory. Amen.

Test yourself: What does the word "amen" mean? Is it enough to know your catechism to be a friend of Jesus?

Under the direction of Romain Lizé, Vice President, Magnificat
Translator: Janet Chevrier
Editor, Magnificat: Isabelle Galmiche
Editor, Ignatius: Vivian Dudro
Assistant to the Editor: Pascale van de Walle
Layout Designer: Elena Germain
Production: Thierry Dubus, Sabine Marioni

Original French edition: *Le petit catéchisme de ma communion*
© 2015 by Mame, Paris.

© 2016 by Magnificat, New York • Ignatius Press, San Francisco
All rights reserved.
ISBN Ignatius Press 978-1-62164-125-4 • ISBN Magnificat 978-1-941709-21-4

The trademark Magnificat depicted in this publication is used under license from and is the exclusive property of Magnificat Central Service Team, Inc., A Ministry to Catholic Women, and may not be used without its written consent.

Printed in June 2016 by Tien Wah Press, Malaysia
Job number MGN 16016
Printed in compliance with the Consumer Protection Safety Act, 2008.